300 Incredible Things for Sports Fans on the Internet

Every effort has been made to make this book as complete and accurate as possible. The information is provided on an "as is" basis, and no warranty or fitness is implied. The author, VIP Publishing and M.K. Distributors, Inc. shall assume neither liability nor responsibility to any person or entity with respect to any loss, damage or suitability of the web sites contained in this book.

VIP Publishing
Marietta, Georgia • (800) 909-6505
Distributed by M.K. Distributors, Inc.

ISBN 0-9658668-2-3

Introduction

The Internet and sports are a perfect match. This combination allows timely delivery of information as well as the thorough, detailed data that can be absorbed at one's own pace. Sports is entertainment, and the Net helps increase the entertainment value for all. So, turn on the Net and let the fun and games begin!

Ken Leebow
Leebow@News-letter.com
http://this.is/TheLeebowLetter

About the Author

Ken Leebow has been in the computer business for over 20 years. The Internet has fascinated him since he began exploring its riches a few years ago, and he has helped thousands of individuals and businesses understand and utilize its resources.

When not on the Net, you can find Ken playing tennis, running (somehow he even ran the New York Marathon), reading or spending time with his family. He is living proof that being addicted to the Net doesn't mean giving up on the other pleasures of life.

— Dedication —

To my favorite baseball player and boyhood hero: Willie Mays (the "say hey kid").

http://www.orst.edu/~protherj/bbl/mays.html
http://www.achievement.org/autodoc/page/may0pro-1
http://www.sfgiants.com/HISTORY/GREATEST/mays.html

Acknowledgments

Putting a book together requires many expressions of appreciation. I do this with great joy, as there are several people who have played vital roles in the process:

- My kids, Alissa and Josh, who helped identify some of the cool sites.

- My wife, Denice, who has been patient with me while I have spent untold hours on the Internet.

- Paul Joffe and Janet Bolton, of *TBI Creative Services*, for their editing and graphics skills and for keeping me focused.

- The multitude of great people who have encouraged and assisted me via e-mail, particularly Kristina Runciman, who serves as copy editor of my weekly e-mail newsletter.

- Mark Krasner and Janice Caselli for sharing my vision of the book and helping make it a reality.

TABLE OF CONTENTS

TABLE OF CONTENTS (continued)

CHAPTER I
KNOW THE SCORE AND MORE

1
Gather All Ye Friends

http://learn2.com/05/0543/0543.html
http://learn2.com/05/0542/0542.html
http://learn2.com/05/0544/0544.html

You love sports, but you have a friend or loved one who is clueless. Instead of wasting your precious viewing hours explaining the sport, shoot 'em over to the learning sites. You'll thank me for giving you more viewing time and saving you the frustration of explaining an illegal defense, a balk or a safety.

2
Reporting by the Fan

http://www.e-sports.com

Be a part of the action. There's lots of fan participation at this site.

Chapter I: *Know the Score and More*

3
Get in the Zone

http://www.statszone.com
Clear and concise scores, stats and more. I like it like that!

4
Sports Today

http://www.usatoday.com/sports/sfront.htm
http://www.usatoday.com/sports/scores98/scores.htm
USA Today provides excellent sports reporting.

5
Nando Knows Sports

http://www.nando.net/SportServer
For current sports news and scores, you'll want Nando on your bookmark list.

6
Yahoo! It's Time

http://my.yahoo.com
http://sports.yahoo.com
Get your timely scores on any sport. My.Yahoo! makes a great start page.

7
Excited About Sports

http://my.excite.com
http://my.excite.com/channel/sports
Excite, one of the major search engines on the Net, has great sports information. It is timely and best of all you can customize it.

8
The Quest is On

http://www.sportquest.com
Here's your "Virtual Resource Center for Sport Information." There are over 13,000 sites indexed at this site.

9
CNNSI

http://cnnsi.com
http://cnnsi.com/email/weekly.html
Combine CNN and Sports Illustrated and what do you get? Excellent sports reporting. Make this one of your pages for timely and detailed sports news.

10
ESPN

http://www.espn.com
One of the best sports sites on the Net. This site will keep you up-to-date when it comes to sports.

11
CBS on the Net

http://www.sportsline.com
This is a winner in the sports and information business. CBS has all kinds of sports information to keep you current.

12
<u>NBC Sports</u>

http://www.nbcsports.com
NBC wants to keep you updated about the sporting world.

13
<u>Fox Sports</u>

http://www.foxsports.com
Fox will keep you informed about all kinds of sports. You can also participate in a variety of polls and quizzes.

14
<u>Slam Sports</u>

http://www.canoe.ca/Slam/home.html
Canada's home page for sports. You will find some great U.S. sports reporting here, as well.

15
Breaking News

http://www.sportsfeed.com/news
http://www.wire.ap.org/APnews/main.html
Sportsfeed and the Associated Press will provide you with the latest and greatest news.

16
Teach Me

http://www.firstbasesports.com
Teaching the world about sports. At this site, you will find sports dictionaries and—best of all—those bewildering hand signals are explained.

17
Youth Sports on the Net

http://www.infosprts.com
Okay, kids, find out what is happening on the Net when it comes to sports.

18
<u>Extra, Extra...Sports</u>

http://web.sportsextra.com

Get a lot of information about most of the major sports. Detailed reporting on the teams, the players and more. Hey, hang out here for a week.

19
<u>Baseball, Basketball and Hockey</u>

http://www.bigleague.com/blbase.htm

http://www.bigleague.com/basketball97.htm

http://www.bigleague.com/blhockey.htm

Every team in each league is listed. It also has professional sites that relate to that team. It's a home run, three-pointer and hat trick all rolled into one!

20
<u>Your Guide to Sports</u>

http://www.netguide.com/Sports

Netguide will guide you to many fine sports sites online.

21
Mining for Sports

http://home.miningco.com/sports
The Mining Company uncovers many sports sites for you. Go for a visit; no equipment required.

22
Sports Fan

http://www.sfan.com
For the real fan, get real-time scores and some great information on all of the major sports.

23
Sports History

http://www.ultranet.com/~rhickok
Tradition! Without our sports history, we have no foundation. Lots of interesting stuff for us "old folk."

24
<u>Legends of the Game</u>
http://www.cmgww.com/sports.html
If you go there, he'll be waiting. And many other legends will be too.

25
<u>What's on TV Today?</u>
http://www.sportsmenu.com
If you want the TV schedules for football, basketball, baseball, and autoracing, make sure you tune in to the Sportsmenu.

26
<u>Sports Pages</u>
http://www.sportspages.com
If you want a quick reference site to most of the newspapers for sports teams or many of the sports analysts, come to the Sports Page.

27
Let's Get Extreme

http://www.extremefans.com
Follow professional and college sports at this extremely good site.

28
All Sports

http://www.allsports.com
A nice, concise recap of most sports with schedules and results. This site also lets you link to audio feeds of many sporting events using Real Audio.

29
Only Sports

http://www.onlysports.com
Well, that's what this book is about, and that's what this site is good for. Timely pro sports information, statistics, trivia and a lot more.

30
<u>For Kids Only</u>

http://www.pathfinder.com/SIFK
Sports Illustrated loves kids. Go here, and you'll see what I mean.

31
<u>The Sporting News</u>

http://www.sportingnews.com
One of the best when it comes to sports information.

32
<u>Sport's Headquarters</u>

http://www.sport-hq.com
Check out the HQ for some good sports sites to visit.

33
It's in the Mail
http://www.infobeat.com
Get all your sports information e-mailed to you by Infobeat. You can choose basketball, baseball, football, tennis, hockey, golf, NASCAR and more.

34
Sports Search
http://www.oldsport.com
Finally, a sports search site with a comprehensive directory.

35
Sports Around the Globe
http://www.sportsline.com/u/worldwide
Keep informed about sports around the world.

36
<u>Traveling Sports Fanatic</u>
http://www.cs.rochester.edu/u/ferguson/schedules
http://www.cs.rochester.edu/u/ferguson/schedules/cities.html
Go ahead; select a city and a date to find out what sporting event is taking place.

37
<u>Sports Stadium and Arena Sites</u>
http://www.wwcd.com/stadiums.html
http://www.ballparks.com
If you are a sports fanatic, check out these arena layouts and seating charts.

38
<u>Stadiums Around the World</u>
http://www.stadianet.com
Here are the official stadium sites. Tour them at your leisure.

39
Sports Network
http://www.sportsnetwork.com
Most of the sports are covered here, and you can view live scoreboards for many.
It's a sports fan's dream come true.

40
The Sports Celebrity Network
http://www.sportspin.com
The Internet channel for daily athlete news.

41
Beckett Online
http://www.beckett.com
The fun of collecting cards. You'll flip out at this site.

42
Listen Up!

http://drew.audionet.com/sports
If you can't watch or listen to it locally, try the Net. Tons of audio broadcasts await you.

43
They're Hot

http://www.web21.com/ath/ath.chtml
These sports folks are mentioned all over the Net. Find out who they are at "Hot Websites." No doubt, you will be taken to some great sites.

44
New Jersey Style

http://sports.nj.com
Get your current sports information with a little "New Jersey" thrown in.

45
Sports Science
http://www.exploratorium.edu/sports
For the cerebral sports fan. Try it, you'll like it.

46
Take a Trip
http://www.sportstrips.com
Are you really a sports fan? Then take a trip to this site.

47
Ask an Expert
http://www.dejanews.com/categories/sports.shtml
Go to DejaNews and discuss sports with your fellow Netizens.

48
Blast Off With

http://www.eblast.com
Encyclopedia Britannica's Sports Internet Guide. Make sure you click on Sports and Recreation.

49
Ballpark Franks

http://www.ballparkfranks.com
Can't get to the ballpark today? Well, try this site. They don't taste and smell as good as you might like, but you will probably start salivating.

50
Trivia Time

http://www.iis-sports.com
All sports fans love trivia. Here's one: "Who had the winning hit in the Braves vs. Pirates playoff series in 1992? Answer: Francisco Cabrera." I was there, and it was the most exciting sporting event I have ever seen.

51
You Make the Call

http://www.dallascowboys.com
http://www.nd.edu
http://www.yankees.com
http://www.bostonceltics.com

They are "America's teams" to some and are hated by others. Check out the Dallas Cowboys, Notre Dame, New York Yankees and the Boston Celtics.

52
And The Winner Is…

http://www.denverbroncos.com
http://www.flamarlins.com
http://www.nba.com/bulls
http://www.nhl.com/teams/det/sitehome.htm

Everyone loves a champion. Here are some recent ones: Broncos, Marlins, Bulls and Red Wings. Visit their official sites.

53
<u>Orthopaedics</u>

http://www.arthroscopy.com/contents.htm
http://www.medfacts.com/sprtsdoc.htm

If you are reading this book, then most likely you are a weekend warrior. So check out these sites. Click there softly, wouldn't want you to get any injuries.

54
<u>Disabled Sports USA</u>

http://www.dsusa.org/~dsusa/dsusa.html

Sports information for the disabled athlete. Provides links to information, such as, the U.S. Disabled Ski Team, U.S. Electronic Wheelchair Hockey sites, and much more.

55
<u>Sports Games on the Net</u>

http://www.alphasim.com

If you like to play games, then play a whole lot of sports games at this site.

56
Leroy Neiman

http://www.leroyneiman.com
If you are a sports fan, then you know about Leroy's artwork. He's an original.

57
Celebrity Athletes

http://www.celebsite.com/people/catbrowse/athleteindex.html
While this site does not profile very many athletes, you may enjoy the other star sightings.

58
The Amateur Athletic Union

http://www.aausports.org
(AAU) is one of the largest, non-profit, volunteer sports organizations in the United States. A multi-sport organization, the AAU is dedicated exclusively to the promotion and development of amateur sports and physical fitness programs.

59
<u>WWW Women's Sports Page</u>
http://fiat.gslis.utexas.edu/~lewisa/womsprt.html
Contains many links to women's sports pages around the Net.

60
<u>Go Girl!</u>
http://www.gogirl.com
Dedicated to getting women of all ages and fitness levels involved in sports.

61
<u>Not for Men Only</u>
http://www.justwomen.com
Who said, "Sports is for men?" Not at this site.

62
Wall Street Meets Sports
http://www.wallstreetsports.com
This site operates a stock market simulation where athletes have been transformed into securities. Sounds like fun?

63
Can We Chat?
http://www.sportswebboard.com
For your chatting pleasure, there are more than 350 different forums and chat areas for sports.

64
411
http://www.encyclopedia.com
http://www.infoplease.com/sports.html
You'll be pleased with all the information these sites will provide. Wait for a rainout because you'll be spending a few hours here.

CHAPTER II
FIELD OF DREAMS

65
Major League Baseball

http://www.majorleaguebaseball.com
http://www.majorleaguebaseball.com/al
http://www.majorleaguebaseball.com/nl
Our national pastime; check out each team at the AL and NL site.

66
Society for American Baseball Research

http://www.sabr.org
Bet you didn't know about this "secret" society! Nothing is private on the Net, so have some fun and do a little research.

67
Louisville Slugger Museum
http://www.slugger.com/museum/index.htm
The crack of the bat is magic to fans. Now visit this museum that brings baseball to life.

68
Wiffleball?
http://www.wiffleball.com
I have fond memories of playing wiffleball with childhood friends. Check out this site for everything about "plastic backyard baseball."

69
Who's on First?
http://yoyo.cc.monash.edu.au/~mist/Humour/WhosOnFirst.html
I don't know!

"WOW! I CAN SEE THE BALLGAME IN THE REFLECTION IN YOUR EYES!"

70
Baseball City
http://www.geocities.com/Colosseum/Field/6849
It's not a beautiful site, but it sure will delight any baseball fan.

71
Coaches Know All
http://www.webball.com
http://www.coachesedge.com
Learn the intricacies of sports from the coaches. Lot's of informative stuff here.

72
Baseball Archive
http://www.baseball1.com
You've got to love a fan who puts so much work into his Web site. Tons of interesting stuff. Thank you, Sean.

73
Mr. Baseball

http://www.baseball-links.com
On the Net, John Skilton would have to be considered Mr. Baseball. He has links and information to an incredible amount of baseball sites.

74
Bigleaguer

http://www.bigleaguers.com
Lot's of good stuff here, but make sure you check out the 411 section. For example, what does "Worm burner" mean? A batted ball that moves across the ground hard and fast.

75
Put Me in Coach

http://www.littleleague.org
Remember the good old days…baseball without the numbers ($$$$).

76
Baseball Hometown Newspapers
http://www.purebaseball.com
During the Major League season, you can follow the team in its hometown paper.
This site makes it easy for you.

77
Picture This
http://www.iexp.com/~gcascar/baseball
Some of the all-time greats. No need for cards, just go to this site.

78
Ah, The Good Old Days
http://www.brooklyn-dodgers.com
For some old-timers, baseball died when the Dodgers left Brooklyn. No matter,
this is an excellent site for any baseball fan.

79
Black Baseball

http://www.blackbaseball.com
Learn about the Negro Baseball Leagues. History, teams, players and more; it's all here.

80
Baseball Hall of Fame

http://www.baseballhalloffame.org
This site is a hit, a home run, a winner. Okay, just go there.

81
Harry Caray

http://www.wgntv.com/sports/hcaray.html
http://www.cubs/hc.htm
Take me out to the ballgame. Read and listen to the legendary announcer.

82
Baseball Trivia
http://www.heavyhitter.com
Take the challenge: Lots of great questions at this site.

83
The World Series
http://www.totalworldseries.com
Being from Atlanta, this site is near and dear to me. The Braves, the team of the 90s.

84
Movin' on Up
http://www.fanlink.com
http://www.minorleaguebaseball.com
Who are the future stars in baseball? Scout and scour this site for our future heroes.

85
Total Baseball

http://www.totalbaseball.com
Well, the name sort of says it, but for statistics, trivia and a lot of other stuff, this site it totally awesome.

86
Fastball

http://www.fastball.com
One of the major baseball sites on the Net.

87
Cal Ripkin, Jr.

http://www.2131.com
"I want to be remembered as an ironman, a player who went out there and put it on the line every day. I want people to say they couldn't keep him out of the lineup." Cal Ripkin, Jr.

88
Hank Aaron

http://tbssuperstation.com/hankaaron
http://cwws.com/~schubert/aaron.htm
http://www.atlantabraves.com/web/hank.aaron/hank.html
Hammerin' Hank. A tribute to the man who will hold the homerun record…forever.

89
The Babe

http://www.baberuthmuseum.com
http://www.baberuthleague.org
He's got a museum, a baseball league and more named after him.

90
Yaz

http://www.yaz.com
Carl Yastrzemski, the last Triple Crown winner (1967). Check out tons of good information about Yaz, and see who the other Triple Crown winners have been.

91
Baseball Parent

http://users.aol.com/baseparent
Mom and apple pie go quite well with this one. If you are a baseball parent, then this site will be a hit with you.

92
Baseball Stuff

http://www.baseballstuff.com
Guess what? You'll find a lot of stuff here. Baseball fans will not want to miss this site.

93
How Does That Ball Curve?

http://library.advanced.org/11902
Learn about the intricacies of baseball from some smart kids.

94
Homerun Derby

http://baseball.yahoo.com/mlb/hrwatch.html
http://cnnsi.com/baseball/mlb/1998/target61
Maris, Mcgwire, Griffey, and Sosa: Who is the King of the long ball?

CHAPTER III
HOOP IT UP

95
<u>The NBA</u>

http://www.nba.com
http://www.nba.com/teamindex.html
The league's official site. Get to each team quickly by using the "Team Index."

96
<u>All the Teams</u>

http://www.netguide.com/guide/sports/nba.html
Simply and easily, get complete information about all the teams.

97
<u>All the NBA Links in the World</u>

http://members.aol.com/nbalinks/index.htm
No doubt, you will have a ball at this site.

98
Math Meets Basketball

http://www.tsoft.com/~deano

Can math and science be applied to basketball? You bet they can.

99
Ms.Basketball

http://www.dfw.net/~patricia

If you're an NBA fan, don't miss this fan's page. You'll find game results and a lot of other interesting stuff.

100
Alleyoop

http://www.alleyoop.com

No doubt, this is a winning basketball site; hang here for a while.

101
Hoop it Up

http://www.onhoops.com
Let these enthusiastic fans keep you informed about the NBA.

102
History of College Basketball

http://www.businesscents.com/cci
From 1938 to the present, it's all here.

103
Man They're Big

http://www.shaq.com
http://www.kareem.com
Check out these giants of the game: Kareem of the past and Shaq of today.

104
Awesome Baby

http://www.dickvitale.com
Yep, even Dick Vitale has a Web site. I can hear him cheering and screaming.

105
Women's Basketball

http://www.wnba.com
http://www.abl.com
It's official; now there are women's professional basketball leagues. And, of course, there are professional Web sites to go along with them.

106
Still Trotting the Globe…

http://www.harlemglobetrotters.com
Though Meadowlark and Curly retired long ago, the Globetrotters are still playing (and always winning) in venues around the world.

"NO LUCK WITH MY CONTACT LENS, BUT I HAVE FOUND THREE EARRINGS!"

107
<u>Basketball Statistics</u>
http://shell.rmi.net/~doug/NBA.html
On the Net, this is your place to find NBA stats.

108
<u>Mike's Official</u>
http://jordan.sportsline.com
Michael Jordan has his official site here. Lots of good information.

109
<u>Chicago Covers Jordan</u>
http://www.chicago.tribune.com/sports/bulls/ws/0,1246,394,00.html
The Chicago Tribune has a sited dedicated to "His Airness."

110
<u>NBA Web Pages</u>

http://www.glue.umd.edu/~toejam/Sports/NBA.html
A great search engine for NBA information. While the URL sounds a little funky, this is a site you will not want to miss.

111
<u>Basketball Hall of Fame</u>

http://www.hoophall.com
Visit this "shrine of the hardwood."

CHAPTER IV
REACHING THE GOAL (POSTS)

112
The NFL

http://www.nfl.com
The official site. And if you know each team's logo, you can quickly get to its site from this page.

113
All the Teams

http://www.netguide.com/guide/sports/nfl.html
Get complete information about all the teams in the NFL.

114
Monday Night Football

http://www.abcmnf.com
The ABC TV crew is waiting for you.

Chapter IV: *Reaching the Goal (Posts)*

115
<u>Superbowl</u>

http://www.superbowl.com
As the big game gets closer, millions of people check this site out.

116
<u>Teaching Statistics with Sports</u>

http://www.he.net/~budsport/edproj.htm
Make the Monday Night Game of the Week a homework project. It works!

117
<u>Hut, Hut, Hut...Hmmm</u>

http://cdl.uta.edu/football
This site is for the football fanatic only.

118
NFL Fans

http://www.nflfans.com
Check out this well-organized, extensive fan site.

119
USA Football Center Online

http://cybergsi.com/foot2.htm
Get brief but solid college and professional football information here.

120
Dick Butkus

http://www.dickbutkus.com
What does one of the all-time greats do when his career is over? Why, host a great football Web site, that's what!

Chapter IV: *Reaching the Goal (Posts)*

121
Football Statistics and More
http://www.footballtown.com
Get your current pro football statistics here. While you do, check out the great links.

122
Picture This
http://www.geocities.com/Colosseum/Arena/7598
Think you know your football? Try to identify 100 players by their photos.

123
NFL Player Search
http://web4.sportsline.com/u/psearch
Type in a player's name, and get tons of information about him.

Chapter IV: *Reaching the Goal (Posts)*

(See below)

Chapter IV: *Reaching the Goal (Posts)*

124
Follow Pro Football…from Hawaii
http://maxwell.uhh.hawaii.edu/football/football.html
This site, originating from the Islands, tracks the NFL and CFL.

125
Football Around the Globe
http://www.wqd.com/fc/gridiron
You don't believe it? Well, go to the site and click on Ukraine.

126
It's Off to Canton
http://www.footballhalloffame.com
The Football Hall of Fame.

Chapter IV: *Reaching the Goal (Posts)*

127
NFL Hometown Newspapers
http://www.pcola.gulf.net/~tedk1/nfl.html
During the NFL season, you can follow the team in its hometown paper. This site makes it very easy.

128
By the Fan and for the Fan
http://www.proballfan.com
Pro Football by the fan, for the fan. The concept is great, but it is a little light on content.

129
Totally Football
http://www.3sports.com
With over 2,400 links, you may never have time to watch another live game.

130
Get Your Kicks...
http://www.soccernet.com
...at soccer.net.

131
America's Soccer Magazine
http://www.socceramerica.com
Keep informed about soccer with this online magazine.

132
GOOOOOOOOOAL!!!
http://www.mlsnet.com
http://www.fifa.com
From Major League Soccer to the Fédération Internationale de Football Association, it's all here for the soccer fan.

Chapter IV: *Reaching the Goal (Posts)*

"WALK IT OFF."

133
<u>The World Cup</u>

http://www.worldcup.com
The Super Bowl of soccer.

134
<u>Rugby Today</u>

http://www.rugbynews.com
Okay, it's not football or soccer, but it sure looks like a lot of fun.

CHAPTER V
ICE, ICE, BABY

135
The NHL

http://www.nhl.com
http://www.nhlpa.com
http://www.nhl.com/teams/index.htm
The official sites for the league and players. Get to each team quickly by using the "Team Index" feature.

136
All the Teams

http://www.netguide.com/guide/sports/nhl.html
Simply and easily, get complete information about all the teams.

137
Pro Hockey EuroReport
http://www.euroreport.com
Track your favorite Europeans playing professional hockey in North America.

138
Hockey Night in Canada
http://www.hockey.cbc.ca
When it comes to hockey, you know that the Great White North has it all.

139
Kids on the Ice
http://www.yhn.com/contents.htm
This site will fill you in about youth hockey.

140
Hockey Guide
http://www.hockeyguide.com
Over 1200 links to hockey sites on the Net.

141
Hockey from Hawaii
http://maxwell.uhh.hawaii.edu/hockey/hockey.html
No, this is not about Hawaiian hockey. It's a very good site (that happens to originate in Hawaii) of NHL info.

142
The Great One
http://www.gretzky.com
Wayne Gretzky. Need I say more, hockey fans?

143
Roller Hockey
http://www.rhockey.com
I can remember playing it in the driveway as a kid. Now, the sport is a lot more serious and organized.

CHAPTER VI
ACE OF CLUBS

144
<u>Golf</u>

http://www.golf.com
Fore, score and the Internet. Hit the links…about the links.

145
<u>The Majors</u>

http://www.golfmajors.com
The Masters, The U.S. Open, The British Open, The PGA Championship. I can hear the roar of the crowd as they approach the 18th green. Quiet, please.

146
<u>Everything Golf</u>

http://www.ttsoft.com/thor/golflinks.html
And I do mean everything. If golf is your thing, go fore it!

147
<u>The Masters</u>

http://www.masters.org
http://www.augustagolf.com
Go for the green.

148
<u>The World of Golf</u>

http://www.worldgolf.com
Seems like you just can't get enough golf these days.

149
<u>Golf Universe</u>

http://www.golfuniverse.com
Courses, news, trivia and many other resources. Take a swing at it; no mulligans allowed.

150
Tune In to the Golf Channel
http://www.thegolfchannel.com
What's on the tube? Statistics and a hole lot more.

151
Golf Travel and Real Estate
http://www.golfmedia.com
For the golfer with lots of bucks.

152
Ladies and Gentlemen
http://www.pga.com
http://www.lpga.com
The official sites of the PGA tours.

153
The 19th Hole

http://www.19thhole.com
Definitely my favorite hole. There is a lot of good information at this site; cocktails are not included.

154
Golfcourse Plus

http://www.golfcourse.com
This site lists most golf courses, but it has much more. If you enjoy golf, I guarantee you will love this one.

155
Golf Online

http://www.golfonline.com
Here it is, from the publishers of Golf Magazine.

156
CyberGolf

http://www.cybergolf.com
Trivia, golf courses and other fun stuff; it's all here.

157
Trivia Golf

http://www.triviagolf.com
If you are a golf fan, this is a fun trivia site you will not want to miss. Here's a sample: "Who was the modern era player to come closest to winning all of the Grand Slam events in one year? Answer: Ben Hogan."

158
GolfWeb

http://www.golfweb.com
This is an excellent site. If you are a golfer, go here right now.

159
I Golf, You Golf, We all Golf

http://www.igolf.com
At I golf, let's play.

160
Golf Search

http://www.golfsearch.com
Sorry, this site will not find your lost ball, but it will tell you where to find golf-related items on the Net.

161
Take the Tour

http://www.pgatour.com
The PGA has an excellent site for all the golf fans around the world.

162
American Junior Golf Association

http://www.ajga.org
Dedicated to the development of young men and women through competitive junior golf.

163
Tiger Woods

http://www.tigerwoods.com
http://www.websites2000.com/golf/twoods
These sites (and Tiger himself) should be around for a long time. Check out the guy who has given golf a big shot in the arm.

164
Da Bear

http://www.nicklaus.com
Jack Niklaus goes high tech on the Web. If you like Jack, you'll enjoy this site.

165
Golfball

http://www.golfball.com
At least you'll never hit one into the water on the Net. Lots of good resources for you here.

166
What a Joke

http://www.totalgolfer.com/comics/index.html
No, not your game…check out these cartoons.

167
World Championship Golf Tournament

http://www.greenland-guide.gl/gt/icegolf/default.htm
Whether you have ever enjoyed a good game of "ice golf" or not, visit this site from Greenland.

"SHE'S A COMPULSIVE SHOPPER! WHY ELSE WOULD SOMEONE GO TO GARAGE SALES ON A DAY LIKE THIS?"

CHAPTER VII
RAISE A RACKET

168
It's a Grand Slam

http://www.wimbledon.org
http://www.usopen.org
http://www.ausopen.org
http://www.frenchopen.org
Get scores and updates from these major tennis tournaments.

169
The Davis Cup

http://www.daviscup.org
During the Davis Cup, get all the current information. In the off season, get historical information.

170
Pro Tennis

http://www.atptour.com
The Association of Tennis Professionals has all the information you want about the players and the tour. You'll love it.

171
Corel Tour

http://www.corelwtatour.com
And you thought Corel was only a computer software company. Check out lots of interesting stuff about female tennis players.

172
Tennis, Anyone?

http://www.tennisone.com
If you play tennis, this is a site you will not want to miss. News and information, lessons, a newsletter and a lot more.

Chapter VII: *Raise a Racket*

173
Tennis Magazine Online
http://www.tennis.com
All tennis fans will love this site. Take it for a spin.

174
Your Serve
http://www.tennisserver.com
This is a fun site for all tennis players. Lots of good information.

175
Martina Hingis
http://www.geocities.com/Colosseum/Field/8888/martina.html
All about this Swiss (though born in Czechoslovakia) tennis sensation.

"THAT <u>BAND</u> GOES ON YOUR WRIST!"

CHAPTER VIII
NO BIZ LIKE SNOW BIZ

176
Winter Sports Foundation

http://www.wintersports.org
A foundation for people who love to play in the white stuff.

177
Ski Colorado and Utah

http://www.skicolorado.org
http://www.skiutah.com
It's worth the trip; or is that the click?

178
Search the Slopes

http://www.skicentral.com
An index and search engine for skiing and snowboarding sites.

179
CNN Ski Report
http://cnn.com/TRAVEL/ski.report/index.html
Get your weather reports from CNN. While you're there, check out its ski links.

180
Give Me That Accumulation
http://www.snowreport.com
Okay, ski folks, watch the snow report and hope there's lots of it.

181
SkiMaps
http://www.skimaps.com/Archive
Getting excited for ski season? Check out the maps of any resort. This is a must-see site for the ski bum. Happy trails.

182
Send a Card
http://www.skigate.com/postcard/card.asp
Send a ski friend a postcard of the mountains; it's almost like being there.

183
We All Ski at ISKI
http://www.iski.com
Weather, resorts, news, gear and more. It's all here for you.

184
Go Ski
http://www.goski.com
Here's a great site that will inform you in detail about the slopes.

185
Ski
http://www.travelbase.com/activities/skiing/ski_search_map.html
Get information on all the ski sites on the Net.

186
WinterNet
http://petrix.com/ski
http://www.iion.com/WinterNet
Ski lovers: check out the slopes.

187
Cross Country Skiing
http://www.xcskiworld.com
Ease on over to this skiing site.

188
Online Lessons

http://www.skinet.com
Get your lessons and tons of other information here.

189
Designer Skis

http://www.myski.com
Too bad you can't be on the slopes every day. Go here to design your own skis.
Pretend you're about to head for the slopes.

190
Everything Snowboarding

http://www.world.de/indexe.htm
http://www.metro.net/nico7f7/directory.html
http://www.nwi.co.uk/homepages/sean/snowlnks.htm
And I do mean everything!

Chapter VIII: *No Biz Like Snow Biz*

191
Iditarod

http://www.iditarod.com
http://www.dogsled.com
Get your dogs and sleds ready. There's mush to see at these sites.

CHAPTER IX
THE OLD COLLEGE TRY

192
Go, Fight, Win
http://www.dowell.com/dondowell/tcu/fightsng/fsongs.htm
Yep, the fight songs for many colleges are provided here.

193
Nicknames
http://www.afn.org/~recycler/sports.html
Which school has the best one? How about the one most frequently used or the most bizarre? You'll find all the answers here.

194
College Sports News
http://www.collegesportsnews.com
All the college sports fit to print.

195
College Football Hall of Fame

http://www.collegefootball.org

Find out who the hall of famers are and a bunch of other good stuff.

196
College Happenings

http://www.evansville.net/~wajl10

Let a college fan provide you with tons of great information. Even when the season is over, you'll get timely information.

197
Wall-to-Wall Pigskin

http://www.cae.wisc.edu/~dwilson/rsfc

Do you really love college football? If yes, don't pass up this site. Be prepared to stay a while.

198
Totally Awesome

http://www.totalcollegesports.com

If you have a need to be in the know, this is your college sports bible.

199
Final Four

http://www.FinalFour.net

For some, the world stops when "March Madness" arrives. If you are a college basketball fanatic, this site is for you.

200
Coach K

http://www.coachk.com

Yes, Coach Krzyzewski has his own Web site. If you like Duke or collegiate basketball, this is a site you'll want to visit.

201
Coach Bobby
http://www.coachbobknight.com
I haven't even gone to the site yet, but I can already hear the yelling and scream-ing. Watch out for flying objects from Indiana U.'s fiery leader.

202
College Sports Feast
http://www.FANSonly.com
If you enjoy college sports, this site was designed for you.

203
College Insider
http://www.collegeinsider.com
When it comes to collegiate football, baseball, basketball and hockey, this is a site you will not want to miss.

204
NCAA Sports Statistics
http://www.ncaa.org/stats
Get a ton of statistics on many of the NCAA sports.

205
What a Finish!
http://www.nd.edu/~tmandell/finishestable.html
Some of the greatest college football game endings. Remember Flutie to Phelan in '84?

206
College Hockey
http://uscollegehockey.com
Check it out.

207
Athletic Supporter
http://athletenetwork.com
If you're a high school or college athlete, this network wants to assist you.

208
Atlantic Coast Conference
http://www.theacc.com
The ACC has some of the best basketball and football in the country.

209
Atlantic 10 Conference
http://www.atlantic10.org
Here's the official site of the Atlantic 10 Conference.

Chapter IX: *The Old College Try*

210
The Pac 10

http://www.pac-10.org
Can you say Rose Bowl dominance?

211
The SEC

http://www.sec.org
Gators, Vols and more; the Southeastern Conference is consistently one of the strongest college football leagues in the country.

212
The Big East

http://www.bigeast.org
Notre Dame, Miami, Georgetown and some other great university teams can be found at this site.

213
<u>The Big Ten</u>
http://www.bigten.org
Michigan, Ohio State—and even Northwestern—are represented along
with the other members of the Big Ten Conference.

214
<u>The Big Twelve</u>
http://www.fansonly.com/confs/big-12
Visit some of the major college powers at this conference.

215
<u>College Sports Center</u>
http://www.sportscom.com/colsport
If there is a college or conference that we missed in the book, stop by the center.
Any college fan will support this site.

CHAPTER X
GO FOR THE GOLD

216
The Olympic Games

http://www.olympic.org
http://www.olympic-usa.org
It's official — these Web sites, of course.

217
Ancient Olympics

http://olympics.tufts.edu
http://devlab.dartmouth.edu/olympic
Learn all about the Olympics of old (and I do mean old).

218
Olympic Pride

http://www.nagano.olympic.org
http://www.sydney.olympic.org
http://www.slc2002.org
http://www.athens2004.gr
Information about the Olympic games of 1998, 2000, 2002 and 2004.

219
Winter Olympics

http://winter.eb.com
http://www.winterolympics.com
Check out the records for all of the Winter Olympic events and view
current information.

220
Gymnastics

http://www.usa-gymnastics.org
The U.S. Gymnastics team seems to cast a special spell on us—especially during the Olympics. Come on, jump over to this site.

221
Tara Lipinski

http://www.taralipinski.com
And it's a triple lutz and a double toe loop!

222
Landing on My Feet

http://www.strug.com
Kerri Strug charmed millions during the 1996 Olympics.

CHAPTER XI
THE GREAT OUTDOORS

223
<u>Climbing Mt. Everest</u>

http://www.everest.mountainzone.com
Let's be honest; we'll never really get there. But we sure can dream about it.

224
<u>Resort Sports Network</u>

http://www.rsn.com
If you love the outdoors, you will want to check this site out. Any time of year this site will be beautiful. Check out the camera shots of these resorts.

Chapter XI: *The Great Outdoors*

225
<u>It's Extreme</u>

http://www.charged.com
If you like Extreme Sports, make sure you visit this site. Don't forget to bring your headgear along.

226
<u>Adrenaline Online</u>

http://www.extremesports.com
Extreme Sports are not for me to play, but I love watching them. Either way, you'll enjoy this site.

227
<u>More Extreme Sports</u>

http://www.xpcsports.com
Professional sports reporting with a little attitude. There's a whole lot of information, and while you're there, take a timely poll.

228
Go to the Mountain

http://www.mountainzone.com
For skiing, snowboarding, biking, hiking, climbing and even photography, go to the mountain.

229
Get Outdoors

http://www.greatoutdoors.com
Who knows? With the Net, some may never go outdoors again.

230
Hunting and Fishing

http://www.spav.com
This site is dedicated to fishing and hunting enthusiasts around the world.

231
The Outdoor Life

http://www.alloutdoors.com
http://www.outdoor.com
Hunting, fishing and a lot more are here for you.

232
Let's Go Huntin'

http://www.hunting.net
This site has a directory of over 1,500 outfitters and lodges, information on all types of game and a lot of other stuff.

233
Goin' Campin'

http://www.campnetamerica.com
Have fun, and don't forget to pack this site as part of your equipment.

234
Outside Online

http://outside.starwave.com
This site is invigorating. It might even tempt you to get offline and go outside.

235
Serious Sports

http://www.serioussports.com
You'll find information here about: Hang Gliding, Paragliding, Skydiving, Soaring, Western Ranches, Horsepacking, Rock Climbing, Mountaineering, Fishing, Whitewater Rafting and Kayaking, Sea Kayaking, Outdoor Schools and more.

CHAPTER XII
ROUND 'EM UP AND BET THE RANCH

236
<u>Rotisserie Baseball</u>

http://www.rotoball.com
Interested in managing your own (fantasy) team? This is where it's happening.

237
<u>Fantasy Leagues</u>

http://fantasyleagues.miningco.com
The Mining Company can help you find some of the fantasy leagues on the Net.

238
<u>What's Your Fantasy?</u>

http://www.mosey.com
http://www.majorleaguemarket.com
Baseball fantasy at its best.

Chapter XII: *Round 'em Up and Bet the Ranch*

239
Fantasy Football

http://www.smallworld.com
http://www.sportshares.com
http://www.bcsports.u-max.com
http://www.cdmnet.com/fsi/football
Well, all you football fanatics, here's your fantasy come true on the Net.

240
Sports Facts

http://www.sportsfaxnews.com
Sports information for the gamblers.

241
Sports and Betting

http://sports.dbc.com
These two things seem to go hand in hand. Check out the timely scores and the odds at the same time.

242
I'm a Gambling Man
http://www.vegasinsider.com
Here's an inside tip. If you enjoy a little wager, go to Vegas Insider.

243
Sports Handicapping
http://www.sportswire.com
I'll bet you'll enjoy this site. Happy gambling.

CHAPTER XIII
ONLY THE STRONG SURVIVE

244
Float Like a Butterfly…

http://www.theslot.com/ali
I am the greatest! Guess who?

245
HBO Does Boxing

http://www.hbo.com/boxing
Knock yourself out with HBO's Web site devoted boxing. This site offers expert analysis, inside information on the fighters, history of the sport, plus a chance to ask questions of some of the biggest names in boxing.

246
Boxing On The Web
http://www.ipcress.com
No doubt, if you are a fight fan, this is one spot you can count on.

247
Ringside Seat
http://www.boxing.com/boxing/mainmenu.html
This site has a lot of information and great boxing links.

248
Boxing Online
http://www.boxingonline.com
Fight fans, this is your site.

249
It's Crunch Time

http://www.fitnessonline.com
Joe Weider has his fitness publications online here. Get out those weights, and get ready for a workout.

250
Get Big

http://www.getbig.com
http://www.muscle-fitness.com
http://nbaf.com/nbaf/home.html
For you muscle men and women, these are your sites for getting bigger and better.

251
In This Corner...

http://www.wwf.com
http://www.prowrestling.com
Is it sport or entertainment? Fake or not, millions of people watch wrestling.

252
Wrestlemania
http://wcwwrestling.com
Is it real or is it wrestling? You make the call.

253
Wrestling Museum
http://www.wrestlingmuseum.com
Case closed. Of course wrestling is real, and there is even an online museum to prove it.

CHAPTER XIV
WET AND WILD

254
<u>The Internet Waterway</u>

http://www.iwol.com
If it is a sport, and it has to do with water, you'll find it here.

255
<u>The Virtual Flyshop</u>

http://www.flyshop.com
Here's a site dedicated to the beautiful art of fly-fishing.

256
<u>Rowing Down the River</u>

http://www.row2k.com
http://www.rowersresource.com
Get those oars ready. What a great resource for rowing fans.

257
Scuba Diving

http://www.usdivers.com
http://www.scubaduba.com
It's fun, it's beautiful and it's on the Net.

258
Diver's Alert Network

http://www.dan.ycg.org
Can't beat this advice: Dive safely.

259
Under The Sea

http://www.padi.com
Sponsored by the Professional Association of Diving Instructors.

260
Surfin' USA

http://www.surfermag.com
You can read part of the monthly print magazine here, plus find photos and content that might not make it into print.

261
Set Sail

http://www.sailing.org
Let the International Sailing Federation float your boat.

262
Swim Info

http://www.swiminfo.com
Swimming World magazine, SWIM Magazine and Technique, provide a site that has news, calendar, articles, training & technique, statistics and a hall of fame.

263
Water Skiing

http://waterski.net
Whether you barefoot, slalom or wimp around on the usual two skis, you'll learn and have fun at this site.

264
In the Swim of Things

http://www.taper-shave.com
Get NCAA swimming updates—top meet results, team rankings, recruiting details and more.

CHAPTER XV
RUGGED INDIVIDUALISM

265
Running Can Be Addictive

http://www2.bw.edu/~tturpin
Not if you go to this site; you'll never leave your computer. If you are a runner, at least give your mouse some exercise.

266
On Your Mark Get Set

http://www.webrace.com
If you need to find a race anywhere in the world, check this site out. It includes running, triathlons, biking and more.

267
Triathlon Online
http://www.triathletemag.com
Fortunately, you only have to click once to get to this site. However, when you get there, they might request you to click 100 times.

268
Runners Take Your Mark
http://www.runnersworld.com
If you are a runner, this is your site. Check out the time calculator. If I run a 10K in 40 minutes, how long will it take me to run a marathon?

269
Track and Field
http://www.tracknews.com
If track and field sports are your thing, then this is your site. Just do it.

270
Run, Baby, Run

http://www.reebok.com
http://www.nike.com
American staples: Reebok and Nike—just click it!

271
Horse Sense

http://www.freerein.com/haynet
Here is a great resource for the horse lover. Sites, sites and more sites to visit.
Jump right over.

272
Horse Country

http://www.horse-country.com
Need information about horses? Go to the country!

273
The Triple Crown

http://www.preakness.com
http://www.kentuckyderby.com
http://www.nyracing.com/belmont
Run with the best.

274
A Bunch of Bull

http://www.pbrnow.com
No joke, it's the Professional Bull Rider's Association. Go for a quick ride at this site.

275
Rodeo Drive

http://www.prorodeo.com
Take the bull by the horns.

276
The Spokin' Word

http://www.ibike.com
Use this site to keep up with everything related to biking.

277
Rollerblading

http://www.rollerblade.com
Check out the great graphics at this site. And please, put that helmet on.

278
Skateboarding USA

http://www.skateboarding.com
For all the skateboard fans, wheel on over here.

279
<u>Bowling</u>

http://www.pbatour.com
http://www.bowlingmuseum.com
Go for it. Get a strike, or better yet, try for a 300.

280
<u>Rack 'em Up</u>

http://www.billiardworld.com
For the pool table enthusiast. They'll also link you up with other good sites.

281
<u>Check Mate</u>

http://www.chessed.com
I've seen it classified as a sport, so check it out. Play a live game on the Net.

CHAPTER XVI
THE SPEED TO SUCCEED

282
Roadsters

http://roadsters.com
If it has fours wheels and is fast, you'll find it here. Anyone that thinks cars are cool will love this site.

283
SuperCars

http://www.supercars.net
At this site you will find "an organized database of the worlds most exotic, rare and fast automobiles."

Chapter XVI: *The Speed to Succeed*

284
Indy Racing

http://www.indyracingleague.com
It's loud, it's fun and it has a great Web site.

285
Speed World

http://www.speedworld.net
Race on over to this site; news, stats, trivia and much more.

286
NASCAR, Anyone?

http://www.nascar.com
http://www.raceshop.com
Rev up those engines. Here's your site for NASCAR racing.

287
Fantasy NASCAR

http://www.motorsports98.com
Compete in fantasy NASCAR racing here, similar to the way rotisserie
baseball and other fantasy sports are played. This site even donates
money to charities.

288
That's Racin'

http://www.thatsracin.com
You bet it is. Tons of great stuff for the racing fan.

289
Get Your Motor Runnin'...

http://www.racelink.com
Are you a motor sports fan? Zoom to this site for racing news, fantasy leagues,
a chat room, a search engine and even an art gallery.

290
Attention: Racing Fans

http://www.irace.com
http://www.irocracing.com
Racing news & views, fun & games and more.

291
Motor Sports

http://www.theautochannel.com/sports
Just about every type of car, truck and motorcycle racing is covered here.

292
Car and Driver

http://www.caranddriver.com
Read the well-known magazine online.

293
Motorcyle Online

http://www.motorcycle.com
Claims to be "the world's largest and most-read digital motorcycle magazine."

294
CART Online

http://www.cart.com
Championship Auto Racing Teams: current news…all the drivers…it's all here.

CHAPTER XVII
I'LL BUY THAT

295
The Splendid Splinter

http://www.hitter.com
http://www.hitter.com/catalog/indes.html
The greatest hitter of them all. Learn about Ted Williams, and check out his catalog.

296
Logo Products

http://www.logosports.com
Wear the logo of your favorite team on a variety of products.

297
Wanna Buy Something?

http://onlinesports.com
This site has a lot of interesting items to buy. Almost all sports are covered.

298
Sports Equipment

http://www.sportsite.com
Buy any sports item online.

299
Zip on Over

http://www.zip2.com
Zip2 is an amazing site for many things. For sports, it will identify many sporting and recreational locations for you.

300
Tickets Please

http://www.webtickets.com
http://www.ticketmaster.com
No doubt, you love being in on the action. Visit these two sites to get tickets.

List additional incredible things that you discover:

301

Site Name:

URL:

Comment:

302

SiteName:

URL:

Comment:

303

Site Name:

URL:

Comment:

304

Site Name:

URL:

Comment:

305

Site Name:

URL:

Comment:

306

Site Name:

URL:

Comment:

List additional incredible things that you discover (continued):

307

Site Name:

URL:

Comment:

308

SiteName:

URL:

Comment:

309

Site Name:

URL:

Comment:

310

Site Name:

URL:

Comment:

311

Site Name:

URL:

Comment:

312

Site Name:

URL:

Comment:

INDEX (BY SITE NUMBER)

INDEX (BY SITE NUMBER)

INDEX (BY SITE NUMBER)

The Incredible Newsletter

If you are enjoying this book, you can also arrange to receive a steady stream of more "incredible Internet things," delivered directly to your e-mail address.

The Leebow Letter, Ken Leebow's weekly e-mail newsletter, provides new sites, updates on existing ones and information about other happenings on the Internet.

For more details about *The Leebow Letter* and how to subscribe, send an e-mail to:
Newsletter@Mindspring.com

Books by Ken Leebow

300 Incredible Things to Do on the Internet

300 Incredible Things for Kids on the Internet

300 Incredible Things for Sports Fans on the Internet